THE REBEL PUBLISHING HOUSE

Osho Rajneesh

More
Gold Nuggets

Compilation and Editing by Ma Deva Sarito
Typesetting by Ma Rashmi Bharti
Design by Ma Krishna Gopa
Photography by Swami Vijayo, Swami Shivananda, M. F. A.
Paintings by Ma Dhyan Sahajo, B. F. A. , M. A.
Production by Swami Prem Visarjan
Printing by Mohndruck, Gütersloh, West Germany

Published by
The Rebel Publishing House GmbH,
Cologne, West Germany

Copyright © Neo-Sannyas International
First Edition

ISBN 3-89338-076-0

In loving gratitude to Osho Rajneesh
Rajneesh Foundation Australia

Osho Rajneesh is
an Enlightened Master
of our time.
All the words printed here
are spoken words,
spontaneously addressed
to a live audience.

INTRODUCTION

It was late summer, 1986. For the past nine months, Osho Rajneesh had been traveling the world, in search of a place to settle and carry on his work of transforming human consciousness. He had found only closed doors, fearful politicians, angry and self-righteous representatives of orthodox religions, everywhere he went.

For those of us who had lived with him in the American commune of Rajneeshpuram – or those who had been able to visit Rajneeshpuram regularly – these were times of waiting, of uncertainty, of reevaluation and change. Many of us didn't even know where Osho was from day to day. It was not clear that we would ever be able to gather together with him again.

In August, the news began to filter around the world: Osho was in Bombay, staying in the house of a disciple near Juhu Beach. The living room was spacious enough to accommodate about 60 or 70 people at a time, and evening discourses were happening. No one knew how long this particular situation would continue. But despite all the uncertainties, Juhu Beach hotels began to fill with people from all over the world. The talk around hotel pools and restaurants was of old times and the times in between, of encounters with the "real world" outside and its joys and sorrows, news of common friends, tearful and joyous reunions. Osho's discourses were videotaped and shown in a hotel the following evening, so that those who couldn't be accommodated inside that night could gather and listen to his words, see his eyes and his gestures on the screen. He was answering our questions – questions filled with the nitty-gitty issues of life that we had all encountered in the times of upheaval just past.

These discourses in Bombay had a quality of the essential – something about the extraordinary events of the past year, the uncertainty of the future, and the sweetness of the present moment combined to make us sharpen our questions, to dig deep for what it was that we really wanted to know. We could not take it for granted that we would be able to ask tomorrow. And Osho's responses reflected and enhanced that essential quality – as always, meeting us where we are and pointing to the skies beyond.

This book is the essence of the essence. For those who already know and love Osho's words, each passage will be a reminder of the whole ocean. And for the newcomers, a taste of the salt and the sweet and all the flavors in between, contained in this one extraordinary human being – who gives us all, without distinction, such immense respect that he can say this:

"One's buddhahood is one's essential nature. I don't want you to worship buddhas, I want you to become buddhas. That is the only right worship. If you love it, become it."

Ma Deva Sarito
June, 1989.

These are the moments, the interval.
Night has gone, the sun will be rising soon.
Make these gaps as beautiful as possible – full of
silence, full of gratitude, gratitude to the
existence that has given you the chance,
gratitude towards all those who have helped.
And wait.

'Wait' is a key word.

You cannot force existence to do things;
you have just to wait.

In the right moment things happen.

You have sown the seeds, you are watering
the garden; now wait. Any hurry is dangerous.
Everything, to grow, takes its time. Only falsities
can be manufactured quickly, in an assembly
line. But realities grow, and growth needs time.

And the inner growth is the greatest growth
in the whole of existence.

The inner and the outer are parts of one reality.

First you have to cleanse the outer, which has been distorted by centuries. It is fortunate that nobody can distort your inner reality; nobody can enter there except you. You cannot even invite your lover, your friend. Except you, you cannot take anyone there. It is fortunate; otherwise everything would have been spoiled in you and recovery would have been impossible.

Only the outer side is covered with dust of all kinds; a small understanding can make you free of it. But that is an essential part – the negative part – to know the false as false, because the moment you know it is false, it drops, it disappears.

And after that the inner journey is very light, very simple.

Awareness is never lost. It simply becomes entangled with the other, with objects.

So the first thing to be remembered: it is never lost, it is your nature, but you can focus it on anything you want. When you get tired of focusing it on money, on power, on prestige, and that great moment comes in your life when you want to close your eyes and focus your awareness on its own source, on where it is coming from, on the roots – in a split second your life is transformed.

You can see that one day is sandwiched between two nights, and you can also see two beautiful days sandwiching one small night.

Choose how you want to feel – to be in heaven or hell.

It is your choice.

The only problem is being in the mind. And the only solution is to get beyond mind. I call it meditation.

There is only one step, and that step is of direction, of dimension. Either we can be focused outside or we can close our eyes to the outside and let our whole consciousness be centered in.

And you will know, because you *are* a knower, you *are* awareness. You have never lost it. You simply got your awareness entangled in a thousand and one things.

Withdraw your awareness from everywhere and just let it rest within yourself, and you have arrived home.

You are always given a single moment; you are not given two moments together. If you know the secret of living one moment you know the whole secret of life, because you will always get one moment – and you know how to live it, how to be totally in it.

Don't go against nature. Listen silently – and whatever you have to do and whatever you have to be, all directions are within you.

5

Meditation is such a mystery that it can be called a science, an art, a knack, without any contradiction.

From one point of view it is a science because there is a clearcut technique that has to be done. There are no exceptions to it, it is almost like a scientific law.

But from a different point of view it can also be said to be an art. Science is an extension of the mind – it is mathematics, it is logic, it is rational. Meditation belongs to the heart, not to the mind – it is closer to love. It is not like other scientific activities, but more like music, poetry, painting, dancing. Hence, it can be called an art.

But meditation is such a great mystery that calling it 'science' and 'art' does not exhaust it. It is a knack – either you get it or you don't get it. A knack is not a science, it cannot be taught. A knack is not an art.

A knack is the most mysterious thing in human understanding.

Meditation, in the last resort, is a knack, too. That's why for thousands of years people have been meditating, teaching, but very few people have achieved heights in meditation. Very few people have even tried. And the vast majority of humanity has not even bothered to think about it.

It is something...a seed you are born with. If you don't have the seed, a master can go on showering all his bliss on you, still nothing will happen in you.

And if the seed is there, just the presence of the master, just the way he looks into your eyes, and something of tremendous importance happens in you – a revolution that you cannot explain to anybody.

If a man has not something in his heart already – a small seed – then it is impossible for him. He can learn the technique, he can learn the art. But if the knack is missing he is not going to succeed.

So thousands of people start meditation, but very few – so few that they can be counted on ten fingers – ever achieve to enlightenment. And unless meditation becomes enlightenment, you have simply wasted your time.

The very essence of meditation is to be so silent that there is no stirring of thoughts in you, that words don't come between you and reality, that the whole net of words falls down, that you are left alone.

This aloneness, this purity, this unclouded sky of your being is meditation.

And meditation is the golden key to all the mysteries of life.

You are aware of objects.

You have to be aware of your subjectivity. When you are looking at a sunset, you are so absorbed in the beauty of the sunset that you completely forget that there is a greater beauty which is making it possible for you to know the beauty of the sunset – it is your awareness. But your awareness is focused on an object – the sunset, the sunrise, the moon.

Drop the object and just remain engulfed in pure awareness, in silence, in peace.

Just be alert.

If you are courageous, listen to the heart.
If you are a coward, listen to the head.
But for the cowards there is no paradise.
Paradise opens its door only for
the courageous.

Everybody is full of love.
If there are no hindrances, the springs
of love start flowing in all directions, without
any address.

Be grateful to existence, enjoy the beautiful
life that surrounds you.
Love – because tomorrow is not certain.
Don't postpone anything beautiful
for tomorrow.
Live intensely, live totally, here and now.

Nobody wants to stand naked in the street. It is better to be miserable – at least you have something to wear, although it is misery...but there is no harm; everybody else is wearing the same kind of clothes. For those who can afford it, their miseries are costly. Those who cannot afford it are doubly miserable – they have to live in a poor kind of misery, nothing much to brag about.

So there are rich miserable people and poor miserable people. And the poor miserable people are trying their hardest to reach somehow to the status of rich miserable people. These are the only two types available.

The third type has been completely forgotten. The third is your reality, and it has no misery in it.

Blissfulness is not something to be achieved. It is already there, we are born with it. We have not lost it, we have simply gone farther away, keeping our backs to ourselves.

It is just behind us – a small turn, and a great revolution.

To know by experience is a risk. You may burn your fingers in the experiment. In the experiment, you are dropping out of the crowd and moving alone in this vast universe and you

don't have any guide, any maps, any instructions. All that you have is a thirst.

Don't create obsessions in your life. Live more playfully, less seriously. Don't be rigid; these are the qualities of the dead. Be flexible. Grow a sense of humor so that you can remain protected from all kinds of dark nights, dark holes. Your sense of humor will protect you.

And if once in a while you can have a deep laughter, from your very roots, it will give you a freshness, a new vitality, a new energy to move mountains.

Never think of going somewhere. Think in terms of transforming yourself here. "There" is a cunning strategy of the mind to deceive you. The mind always makes you interested in things far away, there, so that you can be led away from here. Or at least your attention is no longer here, it is there.

And you will never be there.

Going from here to there, slowly slowly you acquire the habit of always looking there, so wherever you reach, that place is no longer in your focus; your goal has shifted somewhere else.

In India there is an ancient proverb: **Diya tale andhera** – "There is darkness under the lamp." The lamp gives light all around, and just exactly underneath it there is darkness.

This is the situation of man. You are capable of seeing everywhere, all around, but you are incapable of seeing where you are, who you are.

So cancel all the tickets you have booked!

There is nowhere to go; just being here is so blissful.

Close your eyes, so that you can see the reality of the here.

Then and there are only fictions.

Here and now are the only realities.

This is the reason why man is not meditative: The whole society forces him to be in a state of mind, not in a state of meditation.

You were born as nobody and you will die as
nobody.
And between these two points of nobodiness
you remain nobody, just deceiving yourself that
you are this and you are that.

The urge to create anything is the first ray of light in the dark night of your soul. The urge to create is the urge to participate in the work of God.

There is no God as a person, but there is tremendous creativity going on all over the place. God is not a creator to me. God is all this creativity – and whenever you feel some urge to create it is an urge to meet God. It is an urge to be a small God in your own right.

Only by creating something you can feel fulfilled.

Remember only one thing: creativity has two possibilities. One is that it arises out of your silence, love, understanding, your clarity of vision, your intimate friendliness with existence – then creativity is healthy. But if it does not arise out of meditation, out of silence and peace and understanding and love, then there is a danger. It may be arising out of your confused mind, it may be arising out of your insanity.

Anything that comes out of your tense mind, helps you anyway. It gives a relief. Something that was going round and round inside you – you have released it, but it will torture somebody else. It may torture many...because the song that was imprisoned within you was a personal matter. You have made it public, and if the song has come out of some kind of madness, some kind of confusion, you will certainly feel good but at a cost which is too big. Millions of people for thousands of years can be affected by it. You are relieved, but you have not behaved responsibly.

You have not behaved sanely, you have not behaved humanely. Your songs, your paintings, your dance, will have all the qualities of your mind from which they came.

Before you start making your songs and singing and dancing, create the right consciousness, the right awareness, so that whatever comes out of you is a blessing for humanity, not a curse. That is the criterion. Unless it can be a blessing, throw it into the fireplace. You are released, but don't burden somebody else.

If you remain in the mind you can only go mad – that is the ultimate possibility, the ultimate evolution of the mind. If you don't want to go mad, then you will remain simply middle class. And by 'middle class' I mean compromising here, compromising there, a little bit listening to this part, a little bit listening to that part – shattered in fragments, never having an individuality, never having a soul.

Mind and meditation cannot coexist. There is no question of having both of them. Either you can have mind or you can have meditation, because mind is thinking and meditation is silence. Mind is groping in the dark for the door. Meditation is seeing – there is no question of groping, it knows the door.

All great artists, scientists, philosophers, mystics, poets, painters – they are all misfits. And to find a man who is a misfit is to find a man of beauty, of courage, of intelligence...a man who is ready to stand alone against the whole world. The very situation brings out the best in him. He functions at the highest level of being, he functions at the optimum – he **has** to function, because the whole world is against him....

In the whole history of man you can count on your fingers the names of those who have fought against the world. And the very fight has made them a light unto themselves.

If you want to be acquainted with yourself you have to learn the simple art of being silent. The moment you are perfectly silent, life goes through a radical change. Beautiful moments come to you even now, but they are only moments – you become aware and they are gone. You always see them going. You always see their backs, they are putting on their shoes.

You have to be a little more alert.

If you are living a somnambulistic life, almost asleep, then your life is predictable because you are not using consciousness. You are being dominated by unconscious forces within you, and those forces don't have eyes – those forces are blind.

It is because of this that there are things like astrology, palmistry, the I Ching, and a thousand other methods and scriptures. They depend on your mechanicalness.

Any action done unconsciously is a mechanical act, done under mechanical laws. Then you have destiny.

Any action done with consciousness is beyond the powers of mechanical, robotlike functioning. Any act done with alertness is beyond the powers of "destiny."

And that's why we call the man who is enlightened, liberated – liberated from the chains of destiny.

A life is such that it is never complete. A thousand and one things are always incomplete. If death were to wait for you to complete your things, nobody would have ever died.

If I have to choose between gossips and gospels, my preference is for gossips. They are juicier, more alive.

Gospels look sad, dead, heavy. If you have to listen you can manage to listen, but it is not a dance of your heart.

Gossip as aesthetically as possible, as religiously as possible! And gossip something beautiful, something ecstatic.

Lazy people have never done any harm to anybody – they cannot. They will not go through that much trouble.

The active people have created Nadirshah and Genghis Khan and Tamerlane, Adolf Hitler and Joseph Stalin and Mussolini and Ronald Reagan. The world needs to get rid of these active people.

And nobody writes about the lazy people, there is no history about them. There must have been lazy people in the world, but nobody writes any history about them.

They are the very salt of the earth.

Only the man who knows how to meditate is the man who knows how to listen. Or vice-versa: the man who knows how to listen knows how to meditate, because it is the same thing.

Power-hungry people are psychologically sick people. They are suffering from an inferiority complex; they are feeling a wound deep in themselves. They want to be in power to convince themselves that they are something, and to convince you that you cannot take them as ordinary, they are extraordinary people.

And remember, this is the most ordinary desire, to be extraordinary – a very ordinary, common desire found in everybody.

The only extraordinary person is one who has no desire to be extraordinary, who is completely at ease with his ordinariness.

I certainly am a murderer. And also, I never do a thing, so I am a murderer of a very strange category. Just like the candle, and the moth comes towards it, dancing, and dies on its own accord; the candle does not do anything, but certainly it kills.

The whole function of the master is to create such energy, such a magnetic force that you are pulled in and slowly slowly start disappearing. And a point comes when you have become one with existence. This I call **real** death.

Every truth has to be sugar-coated;
otherwise you cannot swallow it.
Buddha said to people, "When you come to your
innermost point, you will disappear – **anatta,**
no-self, no being, no soul. You will be just a zero,
and the zero will be melting into the universal
zero." Very close to the ultimate truth, but told
in a very crude way.

Now, who wants to become a zero? People
have come to find eternal bliss. They are already
tired, miserable, in deep anguish, suffering all
kinds of insanity. And they come to the master
and the master says, "The only medicine is that
you become a zero" – in other words, the disease
can be cured only if the patient is killed.
Translated exactly, that is what it means.

Naturally the disease will disappear when the
patient is killed, but you had come to be cured,
not to be killed!

The religion disappeared within five centuries.
It has intrinsic reasons, and the basic reason
is that people did not find it tasteful, alluring,
attractive. It was naked and true, but who wants
naked truth?

I have to talk about bliss, about benediction,
about thousands of lotuses blossoming in you.
Then you think that it is worth it, just sitting
silently for one hour every day. If thousands of
lotuses open inside, thousands of suns rise, then
it is worth it to find one hour in twenty-four
hours.

But the truth is, no lotuses, no suns – just
pure nothingness.

The moment you come in contact with a master you start dying.
It is a slow process. It is so slow that you are not aware of it. You become aware of it only when you come to a place which I call the point of no return – from where you cannot return, because almost three-fourths of you is dead. Even if you return, people will think you are a ghost! Nobody is going to recognize you again.

Truth knows no fifty-fifty.
It has to be a hundred percent pure; otherwise it is worse than a lie.

If you put zero on one side and hell on another side, people would rather go to hell – at least there they can find some restaurant, some disco. Something is bound to be there, because all the nice people have been going to hell. Only dry bones, so-called saints with no juice at all, are going into heaven. All juicy people – poets, painters, sculptors, dancers, actors, musicians – they are all going into hell.

So if you have a choice between zero and hell, anybody who has any intelligence will choose hell, willingly. But zero...? From hell there is a possibility to get out one day, even to reach to heaven. But from zero, nothing is left, not even a xerox copy – gone, gone, gone forever.

All over the world, whenever you tell people to meditate, they immediately ask, "On what?" because verbally, meditation is action, activity. On what has one to meditate?

Meditation begins only when there is nothing to meditate upon, when there is simply consciousness – you are aware – but you are not concentrating on anything.

In the beginning silence feels like sadness, because you have always been active, engaged, busy – and suddenly all your activity, all your busyness-without-business, all your doings, are gone. It feels as if you have lost everything, your whole life. It looks like sadness.

But just be a little patient – let this sadness settle. This is the beginning of silence.

As sadness settles, you will start enjoying the peace, the inactivity, no turmoil...and a point will come where you will see that it was a misunderstanding: it was silence, but you misunderstood it as sadness. You just have to become acquainted with it. A little deeper friendship with what you are calling sadness and the same sadness will become your deep, cool silence.

Life is boring – so there is no harm in sitting with closed eyes, because there is nothing to see. Sit silently, peacefully.

You have looked outside and you have found nothing but meaninglessness. Now give a chance to your inner world: look inwards. And I promise you that the same eyes which have not found anything outside will find inside **everything,** a constant hallelujah.

The first principle of an authentic religious man is to accept himself as he is, without any judgment – and only from there does your authentic pilgrimage begin.

My work is to make you more and more aware, and when you become more aware you become aware of more problems.

Those problems were there before.

I don't create your problems, it is just that you were unconscious, you were not taking any note. Those problems were there.

It is just like a house which is in darkness, and many spiders are weaving their nests and scorpions are living and snakes are enjoying, and suddenly you bring the light there. The light does not create the spiders or the scorpions or the snakes, but it makes you aware of them.

And it is good to be aware, because then the house can be cleaned; then you can avoid the snakes.

If you only listen to that which is said, you are a student. You listen to the words, you miss the wordless.

The moment you start listening to the wordless, you are initiated into disciplehood.

Growing old, any animal is capable of. Growing up is the prerogative of human beings.

Only a few claim the right.

Enjoy your body, enjoy your physical existence. There is no sin in it. Hidden behind it is your spiritual growing, is your spiritual blissfulness.

When you are tired of physical pleasures, only then will you ask, "Is there something more?" This question cannot be only intellectual, it has to be existential: "Is there something more?"

And when the question is existential, you will find within yourself something more.

There is something much more. Zorba is only the beginning.

Once the Buddha, the awakened soul, takes possession of you, then you will know that pleasure was not even a shadow. There is so much bliss…. That bliss is not against pleasure. In fact, it is pleasure which has brought you to bliss.

There is no fight between Zorba and Buddha. Zorba is the arrow – if you follow it rightly, you will reach the Buddha.

I am not a man of words.
Although I have spoken more words than anybody else in the whole world, still I say I am not a man of words. My words are just like nets thrown to catch fish.

My message is wordless.

Life is a mystery.

Here, the people who are non-vegetarians, drunkards, gamblers...you may find them so loving and so human that it is surprising. And on the other hand, the people who are strictly vegetarian... Adolf Hitler was strictly vegetarian. He never smoked, he never drank any alcoholic beverage, he went to bed early, he got up early in the morning – he was a saint! If you just look at his life-pattern and style, he was a monk. And he killed six million people. It would have been better if he had been a drunkard, non-vegetarian – a chain smoker, but a nice human being.

I am for man's spiritual growth, but I understand spiritual growth in its whole context. It is not something separate, one-dimensional; it is a multi-dimensional phenomenon. It needs a revolution in society. It needs a revolution in society's economic, political structures; it needs a tremendous and radical change in everything that has been dominating us up to now.

We have to create a discontinuity with the past.

Only then a new man – a really spiritual man, a man of cosmic dimensions – can be born.

What is a mystic? – one who knows no answer, one who has asked every possible question and found that no question is

answerable. Finding this, he has dropped
questioning. Not that he has found the answer –
he has simply found one thing, that there is no
answer anywhere.

Life is a mystery, not a question. Not a puzzle
to be solved, not a question to be answered,
but a mystery to be lived, a mystery to be loved,
a mystery to be danced.

Science has no right to deny consciousness
unless it has explored the inner sky of human
consciousness and found that it is dream stuff,
not a reality but only a shadow. They have **not**
explored – they have simply assumed.

Materialism is the assumption, the superstition
of the world of science, just as God, heaven and
hell are superstitions of the religious world.

There is only one basic fear. All other small
fears are by-products of the one main fear
that every human being carries with himself –
the fear of losing yourself. It may be in death,
it may be in love, but the fear is the same:

You are afraid of losing yourself.

And the strangest thing is that only those
people are afraid of losing themselves who don't
have themselves. Those who have themselves
are not afraid.

J ust look all around.
Look at the ocean, look at the sky.
How can you manage not to be simple
and not to be humble?

In the world it is being taught to everybody that losing the mind is madness. It is not the whole truth, because no madman ever loses his mind; in fact, the madman is lost in the mind — his mind has become a jungle and he cannot find his way out of it. It is not that he has lost his mind, he is lost in his mind. He is more mind than he ever was before.

The madman has more mind than you have. Your mind is not so uncontrollable, not so big, not so fast; it is a normal size, manageable. The madman has lost himself in vast, unlimited thoughts, desires, dreams.

So the maxim that "losing the mind is madness" is not right; it has to be changed. Losing yourself in the mind is madness.

And if you understand this, then the definition of sanity is simple: coming out of the mind into the open, into the silence, where no thought, no desire disturbs you.

You are just a pool of silence, not even a ripple on it — this is sanity.

Every generation goes on giving its diseases to the coming generation.
My people have to be aware and alert not to pass on any sickness which they may have received from the past generation.
Let this be the dead end.

Truth is infectious, and there is no antidote to it yet.

Anybody who has ears can hear, but it is not necessary that he will be able to listen. For listening, something more is necessary than just having ears: a certain kind of silence, a serenity, a peace – the heart standing behind the ears, not the mind.

It is the mind which makes you almost deaf, although you are not deaf, because the mind is constantly chattering; it is a chatterbox. Just sometimes sit in your room, close your doors, and write down whatsoever comes in your mind just to see what goes on in it. Don't edit it – because you are not going to show it to anybody, so just write down exactly what comes to your mind. And you will be surprised: just within ten minutes you will see that you are not sane; your mind is the mind of an insane person.

Just somehow you are managing, covering it up, not allowing anybody to know what goes on inside you. And you have become experts, so much so that it is not only that you don't allow others to know what goes on in your mind, you yourself don't see it. And it goes on, yakkety-yak, yakkety-yak.

Because of this constant mind, making noise...although you are not deaf, you cannot listen. You can hear.

Hearing is possible for everybody.
Listening is possible only for those who are silent.

There are things which only **happen**, which cannot be done.
Doing is the way of very ordinary things, mundane things. You can do something to earn money, you can do something to be powerful, you can do something to have prestige; but you cannot do anything as far as love is concerned, gratitude is concerned, silence is concerned.

It is a very significant thing to understand that doing means the world, and non-doing means that which is beyond the world – where things happen, where only the tide brings you to the shore.

If you swim, you miss.

If you do something you will undo it; because all doing is mundane. Very few people come to know the secret of non-doing and allowing things to happen.

If you want great things – things which are beyond the small reach of human hands, human mind, human abilities – then you will have to learn the art of non-doing.

History consists only of daily newspapers, collected, just superficial. It does not give insight.

This is the distinction between dream and reality:

Reality is that which remains as it is. Dream is something that happens once and is gone. And it is not in your hands to bring it back, you cannot manage to dream it. Every morning you will open your eyes – your room will be the same. Every night you will close your eyes – your dreams will be different. That which remains the same is the real, and that which goes on fleeting, changing, and is not under your control, is a dream.

Don't waste your time in dreams.

If you can get rid of God you are mature. According to me, twenty-one years of age does not make you mature, adult. Only one thing makes man mature, and that is getting rid of God – because God is a bundle of all kinds of fears, greeds, hopes. It is opium, it keeps you drugged. But while you are drugged your life is slipping by, and soon death will knock on the door and then it will be too late.

To find the real answer to the question you have to sit silently, alert, not falling asleep, and just going inwards, slowly slowly....

First it will start becoming darker and darker and darker, and then suddenly there is dawn, and the birds are singing and the sun is rising and you are free.

Your wings are open for the first time. Now you can claim the whole sky with all its stars.

A man without God is an authentic man.

Wherever there is life, wherever there is consciousness, there is god. And when you come to the ultimate experience of consciousness you become a god. Everybody's birthright is to become a god – not to worship God but to become a god.

The difference between trusting and being naive is vast, yet the dividing line is very subtle.

Being naive means being ignorant. Trusting is the most intelligent act in existence. And the symptoms to be remembered are these: both will be cheated, both will be deceived, but the person who is naive will feel cheated, will feel deceived, will be angry, will start distrusting people. His naiveness will sooner or later become distrust. And the person who trusts is also going to be cheated, is also going to be deceived, but he is not going to feel hurt. He will simply feel compassionate towards those who have cheated him, who have deceived him, and his trust will not be lost. His trust will never turn into distrust of humanity.

These are the symptoms.

In the beginning they both look the same. But in the end, the quality of being naive turns into distrust, and the quality of trusting goes on becoming more trusting, more compassionate, more understanding of human weaknesses, human frailties. The trust is so valuable that one is ready to lose everything, but not the trust.

Remember one thing: that you should not leave this earth unless you have made it a little more beautiful, a little lovelier, a little more loving.

To me, this is the only strength, the only power – that we can transform life, we can transform consciousness.

Accept it peacefully and joyously, wherever you are, whatever you are, however you can use your energies in some creativity.

We are not searching for any paradise in the clouds. If it is there, we will get hold of it, but first we have to make a paradise here on the earth; that will be our preparation. If we can live in a paradise on the earth, then wherever paradise is, it is ours.

Remember one thing:
Unless the truth is your own experience, whatever you believe about truth is only a belief. And all beliefs are lies, and all believers are blind.

In my way of looking at things, mind itself is sick. Unless you get out of it, you cannot help the poor mind to become healthy. You are too much identified.

Not being identified with the mind is the shortest way to your own being. And your being is always healthy, it does not know what sickness is. It cannot know, it is not in its nature.

Just as mind cannot know peace, your being cannot know tensions, anxieties, anguish. The question is not of curing the mind, the question is shifting your whole energy, your whole focus, from mind to being.

Meditation helps you to shift.

This great shift of your attention, of your awareness, is what I call the psychology of the buddhas.

Everybody has to find out what is close to his heart.
I am speaking for many people of many types.

You have to find out what is right for you. If you start doing **everything** that I am saying you will get in a mess! You simply do that which your heart supports.

You are not using your potential in its totality; you are using it only partially, a very small part, a fragment. And if you are not using your potential in its totality, you will never feel fulfilled. That is the misery, that is the cause of anguish.

You are born to be mystics. Unless you are a mystic, unless you have come to know existence as a mystery – beyond words, beyond reason, beyond logic, beyond mind – you have not taken the challenge of life; you have been a coward. You have wings, but you have forgotten it.

Once you are enlightened, you can use the mind the way it is meant to be used, as a beautiful computer. And because you are enlightened it is no longer clouded with sentiments and emotions; it is clean, a sky without any clouds.

Its clarity is its genius. And every mind is a genius, there are no other kinds of minds in the world.

My love is simply love – neither more nor less. I cannot figure out how to love less. I have tried! – but I am ashamed to say to you that I have failed continuously for my whole life. I have not been able to love less, and neither can I love more. 'More' and 'less' are words that don't belong to the spiritual realm. They belong to the world of matter.

The English word 'matter' is from a Sanskrit root, **matra.** It means "that which can be measured."

That which can be measured is not my love.

That which cannot be measured, that which cannot be more or less, that which is just for you to share....

Because this whole existence is made of the stuff called love. As you understand your reality, you have understood in miniature the reality of the whole existence – it is made of the matter called love.

We are living in an ocean of love, unaware.

Remember, 'duty' is a four-letter word. Love knows no duty. It does many things, but it loves to do them – it is not duty.

In all the languages of the world, strangely enough, people use the phrase "falling in love." Without any exception, in all the languages people say, "I have fallen in love."

But why should you fall?

Why can't you rise in love?

If you want a loving relationship then you should forget all power politics. You can be just a friend, neither trying to dominate the other nor being dominated by the other. It is possible only if you have a certain meditativeness in your life. Otherwise it is not possible.

To love a human being is one of the most difficult things in the world, because the moment you start showing your love, the other starts going on a power trip. He knows you are dependent on him, or on her. You can be enslaved – psychologically, spiritually – and nobody wants to be a slave. But all your human relationships turn into slavery.

Love needs a clarity of vision.

Love needs a cleaning of all kinds of ugly things which are in your mind – jealousy, anger, the desire to dominate....

Men and women have to live together on the earth, but they have not learned how to be together and yet not lose their individuality, how to be together so much that they are almost one, without disturbing the oneness in mundane affairs.

Man and woman both can help – and if the right kind of help is available, there will be no need for man to escape to the mountains, to the caves, to the monasteries. There is no need, because you cannot find a better place than your home. A loving atmosphere, people who understand you, people who understand your silence and your meditation, will go hand in hand with your love.

Even if you get into meditation in the mountains, you will have only one wing. You will not be able to fly to the sun. The other wing you have left in the world, which could have been a tremendous help to you, and you could have been a great help in return.

If a couple gets initiated into meditation together, they are really getting married for the first time. As for your other registration certificates for marriage, they are not valid for me. To me, there is only one certificate that existence gives you – where love and meditation have been helping each other, supporting each other, and opening the doors of the sky for your flight, the flight of the alone to the alone.

It is strange that women are fighting for liberation and men are just standing, looking awkward. Do something! You also have to become free. A men's liberation movement is as much a necessity as a women's liberation movement.

In fact, both movements should be two wings of one movement for freedom.

Nobody is made for anybody. But it takes a little time…a few women in your life, a few men in your life, then you understand that it is the same game. Faces change, bodies change, but the game remains the same – and a boring game! Not only boring, but if you keep all the lights on, then disgusting too.

Strange type of thing… Just this game of sex is enough proof that no God has created man, because if this is what God has created then he seems to be really a rascal! Some better arrangement could have been made. But this is the arrangement – that everybody feels ashamed of it, that people go in the dark, turn the light off.

It has to come out of your meditation – only then does love have eyes. Otherwise love is blind. And unless love has eyes, it is worthless. It is going to create more and more trouble for you, because two blind persons with blind expectations are not only going to double the troubles of life, they are going to multiply the troubles of life.

So be silent and be alert. Be loving.

Love neither interferes in anybody's life nor allows anybody else to interfere into one's own life.

Love gives individuality to others, but does not lose its own individuality.

If love arises out of harmony, then only will we know a successful life, a life of fulfillment in which love goes on deepening because it does not depend on anything outer; it depends on something inner. It does not depend on the nose and the length of the nose; it depends on an inner feeling of two hearts beating in the same rhythm.

That rhythm can go on growing, can have new depths, newer spaces. Sex can be a part of it, but it is not sexual. Sex may come into it, may disappear in it. It is far greater than sex.

For a lighter life, for a more playful life, you need to be flexible. You have to remember that freedom is the highest value, and if love is not giving you freedom then it is not love.

Freedom is a criterion:

Anything that gives you freedom is right, and anything that destroys your freedom is wrong.

If you can remember this small criterion, your life will slowly slowly start settling on the right path about everything – your relationships, your meditations, your creativity, whatever you are.

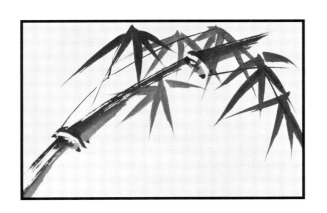

Love is a very new thing in human life. Animals reproduce but they don't love. You will not find in buffaloes Romeo and Juliet, Laila and Majnu, Shiri and Farhad, Soni and Mahival. No buffaloes are interested in such romantic things – they are very earthbound, they reproduce.

And nature is perfectly satisfied with buffaloes, remember. Nature may be trying to destroy humanity, but nature is not trying to destroy buffaloes and donkeys and monkeys, no. They are not problems at all.

Love is a new phenomenon that has arisen with human consciousness. You will have to learn it.

The new humanity has to create the right atmosphere where men and women are friends, fellow travelers, making each other whole. The journey becomes a joy, the journey becomes a song, the journey becomes a dance.

And if men and women in total harmony can give birth to children, those children will be the 'superman' we have been dreaming about for thousands of years.

But the superman can be created only out of the harmonious whole of man's and woman's energy. Then he will be born enlightened.

In the past, people had to seek enlightenment. But if a child is born out of a couple who are in total harmony, in absolute love, he will be born enlightened. It cannot be otherwise. Enlightenment will be his beginning; he will go beyond enlightenment from the very first step. He will seek new spaces, new skies.

Man and woman are two parts of one whole; their world should also be one whole, and they should share all the qualities without any distinction – no quality should be stamped as feminine or masculine.

When you are making love, is your woman really there? Is your man really there? Or are you just doing a ritual, something which has to be done, a duty to be fulfilled?

If you want a harmonious relationship you will have to learn to be more meditative. Love alone is not enough.

Love alone is blind; meditation gives it eyes. Meditation gives it understanding. And once your love is both love and meditation, you become fellow travelers. Then it is no longer an ordinary relationship between husband and wife. Then it becomes a friendliness on the path towards discovering the mysteries of life.

People are taking everything so seriously that it becomes a burden on them.
Learn to laugh more.
To me, laughter is as sacred as prayer.

Suicide is nothing but the last complaint, the ugliest complaint against existence.

Life is a school, and unless you have learned the lesson you will have to come back again and again to the same class. Once you have learned the lesson, passed the examination, then even if you want to come back into the class you will find all doors are closed for you. You have to move to a higher, to a different level of being.
We have moved from one form to another form.

Man is the last form.
Beyond man is a formless, oceanic
consciousness.

Enlightenment is simply realizing one's
universal self. Whoever realizes it has
the same taste – his eyes radiate the same light,
his gestures have the same grace, he has
the same beauty.

If you are receptive, meeting one enlightened
person, you have met **all** the enlightened people
who have happened in the whole history of
man; not only the past, but even those who will
happen in the future.

In the enlightened consciousness the past,
the present, the future, are all dissolved
into a single moment.

Belief is very cheap.
Everybody is a believer – somebody is a
Hindu, somebody is a Mohammedan, somebody
is a Christian. Belief comes in all sizes, all shapes,
all colors – you can choose. And you don't have
to pay anything for it. Generally you get it
with your mother's milk, free of charge.

Life must be a seeking – not a desire, but
a search; not an ambition to become this,
to become that, a president of a country
or a prime minister of a country, but a search
to find out, "Who am I?"

It is very strange that people who don't know
who they are, are trying to become somebody.
They don't even know who they are right now!
They are unacquainted with their being,
but they have a goal of becoming.

Becoming is the disease of the soul.
Being
is you.

Children are born of you, but they don't
belong to you. They belong to the future,
of which you know nothing.

You are the sunset, your children are the
sunrise – and the gap of the whole night is there.

If you love your children, don't give them any belief. Help them so that they can grow trust. If you don't know something, never lie to the children because sooner or later they are going to find that you lied – and when a child finds that the father lied to him, the teacher lied, the priest lied, all possibilities of trust are destroyed. He could not have conceived that the people he has loved – and has loved totally, because a child loves totally....

An innocent child, absolutely dependent on you, and you have the nerve to deceive him, to say things which he is going to find one day that you never knew. If he asks about God, if you are an authentic father, sincere, honest, you should say "I am seeking, I have not found yet." Give your child a desire to seek, a desire to search. Help him to go on a pilgrimage, and tell him, "It may be that you find it before I find it. Then don't forget me; then help me to find it. Right now, I don't know."

Your child will never disrespect you; your child will never come to a point when he will say that you were dishonest towards him, that you lied. And your child will have tremendous honor for you because you made him, his innocence, his questioning, into a search. You created a seeker, not a believer.

Whatever I am saying is so simple, so obvious. There is no question of understanding it; just listening to it is enough. And if it is difficult, that simply means you have not listened.

Forget understanding.

Put your whole energy into listening, and understanding will come on its own accord, just like a shadow that follows you.

Nobody hears the heart.
And the mind is so chattering, so
continuously chattering – yakkety-yak, yakkety-
yak – that even if the heart sometimes says
something it never reaches to you. It **cannot**
reach. The bazaar in your head is buzzing so
much that it is impossible, absolutely impossible
for the heart.

Slowly slowly, the heart stops saying
anything. Not heard again and again, ignored
again and again, it falls silent.

The head runs the show in the society;
otherwise we would have lived in a totally
different world, more loving, less hate, less war,
no possibility of nuclear weapons. The heart will
never give support for any destructive methods
to be evolved. The heart will never be in the
service of death. It is life – it throbs for life,
it beats for life.

Each meeting with an enlightened person
is meeting with a mirror. You see yourself
as in reality you are – not the mask but the
original face, not the personality but your
universal being.

The meeting with the enlightened person
creates a resonance, a certain vibration that
reaches to the very depths of your being.

The ego does not exist.
And you are so identified with the ego that the death of the ego, the disappearance of the ego feels as if it is your death. It is not so; on the contrary, when the ego is dead then you will know your reality, your essential being.

If you can see me, not as a body...if you can see into my eyes, if you can feel my presence, if something stirs in your heart, then certainly you will know that the life you have lived up to now is a life of falsity.

But once you have known even a little bit of the truth you cannot go back. Then there is only one way, and that is to go ahead.

What you have seen in my eyes, others will see in your eyes soon. What you have felt in my presence, others will start feeling in your presence. Because whatsoever I have got, you have got. It is just that you have not unpacked; your suitcases are locked.

Existence is a tremendous experiment in becoming conscious, and man is the pinnacle of the experiment. There are problems, and there are difficulties – but they are the challenges, they keep us alert. They are not ultimately against us, but perhaps they are needed to keep us awake.

All the religions have corrupted your minds because they have not taught you how to watch, how to understand; instead they have given you conclusions – that anger is bad. And the moment you condemn something, you have already taken a certain position of judgment. You have judged; now you cannot be aware.

Awareness needs a state of no-judgment.

And all the religions have been teaching people judgments: this is good, this is bad, this is sin, this is virtue – this is the whole mind crap that for centuries man's mind has been loaded with. So with everything, the moment you see it there is immediately a judgment about it within you. You cannot simply see it, you cannot be just a mirror without saying anything.

Understanding arises by becoming a mirror, a mirror of all that goes on in the mind.

I don't teach you any morality. I don't say "this is good, this is wrong, this is moral, this is immoral" – that is all childish.

I teach you a single criterion: awareness.

If in awareness you do something, it has to be right, because in awareness you cannot do anything wrong. And without awareness you may be doing something very good, appreciated by everybody, but still I say it is wrong because you are not aware. You must be doing it for wrong reasons.

Meditation is not something mental. Meditation is something concerned with your being.

Just plugging into it a little...and suddenly everything is different.

The body will go on in its own way, but you will know that you are not the body. People will die, but you will know that death is impossible. Your own death will come – but meditation prepares you for death so that you can go dancing and singing into the ultimate silence, leaving the form behind and disappearing into the formless.

Mind is the lowest part of your consciousness. It is good as far as the world is concerned, but it is not of any use if you are thinking to go on an inner pilgrimage.

The real and authentic religious search is not of finding, but of losing – the idea of finding is still greed. The idea of finding the truth or God or the ultimate still carries something of greed.

The true mystic, the true religious person, is finding a way to lose himself, how not to be – because those few chosen ones who have attained to the state of 'not to be' have experienced the greatest ecstasy possible.

From 'to be' towards 'not to be' is the pilgrimage.

When I answer your questions it is not that I have got an answer and I simply give it to you. I don't have any answer.

I simply listen to your question and let my silence respond to it; hence, you can find many contradictions in my answers. But I am not responsible, because I have never answered.

It is the silence that goes on responding at different moments in different times to different people in different ways. Just as you listen to the answer, I also listen to it.

There is no speaker here.

Here, there are only listeners.

Channeling is simply a new name for an old disease. In the past they used to call it "being possessed by a ghost."

The modern man has not yet come into existence.
The people in the world are all very old and very ancient. It is rare to come across a contemporary.

Somebody belongs to a religion founded ten thousand years ago, somebody belongs to a religion two thousand years old – these people are not contemporary. They are living in modern times but they are not modern.

And this has created a tremendous problem: technology, scientific progress, needs the modern man to use it. And the modern man is not available. Technology is available, science is available, but the people who can use it creatively are non-existent.

The result is disastrous, because to these people who are not contemporary, science has given technological instruments, machines, which are dangerous. It is like putting a sword in the hands of a child: he is going to hurt somebody, or himself; he is not a swordsman, he is not trained for it.

Man is lagging behind, and the technology has gone far ahead of him. He does not know what to do with it, and whatever he is going to do with it is going to be wrong.

I know you are not beyond pettiness, beyond jealousy, beyond greed, beyond anger. But I don't talk about going beyond them for the simple reason that if you start struggling with your pettiness you will remain petty; if you start struggling against your jealousy, you will remain jealous.

An ancient proverb is: "Always choose the enemy very carefully" – because you will be fighting with him, and in fighting you will become just like the enemy because you will have to use the same methods, the same means.

Enemies are very precious.

I don't want you to fight with small things. Rather than looking down at the earth, and all around is your pettiness and jealousy and anger, my effort is to show you the stars and help you to know that you have wings. And once you start moving towards the stars, those small things will disappear on their own accord.

Every river is constantly moving to be the ocean. The problem is only with those who have become ponds, closed, not open to flow, having forgotten that this is not their destiny, this is death. To be a pond is to commit suicide, because there is no growth anymore, no new spaces, no new experiences, no new skies – just the old pond, rotting in itself, becoming more and more muddy.

To be a seeker means dropping this static state and becoming a changing, moving, flowing river.

It does not matter when you reach the ocean.

The beginning is the end.

The whole beauty is in the beginning, because once you have started moving, the end, falling into the ocean, is absolutely determined. The beginning was in your hands; it was your freedom, hence the beauty of the beginning.

Falling into the ocean will be tremendously ecstatic, but it is not in your hands. What was in your hands was the beginning, and you gathered courage; you jumped out of a static, dead situation into a living being...alive, singing and dancing.

Who cares when the ocean comes?

The beginning is enough, more than enough – because falling into the ocean is bound to happen.

Whenever you understand that you have missed life, the first principle to be brought back is innocence. Drop your knowledge, forget your scriptures, forget your religions, your theologies, your philosophies.

Be born again, become innocent – and it is in your hands. Clean your mind of all that is not known by you, of all that is borrowed, all that has come from tradition, convention, all that has been given to you by others – parents, teachers, universities. Just get rid of it.

Once again be simple, once again be a child.

And this miracle is possible by meditation.

Meditation is simply a strange surgical method which cuts you away from all that is not yours and saves only that which is your authentic being.

It burns everything else and leaves you standing naked, alone under the sun, in the wind. It is as if you are the first man who has descended onto earth – who knows nothing, who has to discover everything, who has to be a seeker, who has to go on a pilgrimage.

The path is very simple.
The path is to get out of the mind as many times in the day as possible. Whenever you have time, just get out of the mind.

A few things can be helpful. If you cannot be silent just by sitting, if you feel too much energy to do something and if you don't do it then the whole energy becomes a mind game, it is easier to begin with some creativity. If you are interested in music, play music, and get drowned in it. If you love dance, dance, and let the dancer disappear.

Or anything – if you know pottery, make beautiful pots, bringing your total energy to it. Because when you bring your total energy to something, mind does not get any energy and becomes silent on its own accord.

And it is only in the beginning that you have to do some work to keep yourself engaged, so the energy moves into that engagement and the mind becomes silent. Soon you will be able to sit silently, doing nothing, and the mind becomes utterly silent.

In those moments you will know the eternity of life, you will know the beauty of this fragile existence around you, and also the great treasure of your own being.

Meditation has two parts: one, a cleaning part. You are going to invite the greatest guest into your life. Clean the whole house, make it pure, fragrant, make it an aesthetic phenomenon inside you.

Catharsis is perfectly good and right, but it is incomplete. After catharsis begins the real work. When you have cleaned the ground of weeds and wild grass, then is the time to sow the seeds of flowers and wait for the spring.

One just needs a little alertness to see and find out:
Life is really a great cosmic laughter. Those who become silent and happy join in the laughter.

Laughter is my message.

I do not ask you to do prayer, I ask you to find moments, situations in which you can laugh wholeheartedly.

Your laughter will open a thousand and one roses in you.

Things are simple. But somehow the mind wants to make them unnecessarily complicated, because unless they are complicated the mind is not of any use.

The mind is useful only when something is complicated – then the mind is needed. When the thing is simple the mind is not needed at all.

And life is so simple that if one is courageous enough to live it, mind can be abandoned completely. And to abandon the mind and to live life spontaneously is what I call sannyas.

If you want to have a rapport with reality, you have to be neither a fool nor shrewd. You have to be innocent. So whatever you bring – skepticism, atheism, theism, communism, fascism, any type of nonsense you can bring here – my medicine is the same.

It does not matter what kind of nonsense is filled in your head when you come here. I will chop your head without any distinction. Who is sitting on your head does not matter – my concern is chopping!

I am just a woodcutter....

Life is simple.
We make it complex by doing things
against nature.

There is only one religion, and that is nature.
Allow nature to take you completely; allow
yourself to be one with nature.

A total human being has not been born yet.
There have been men and there have been
women, but there have not been human beings.

My whole approach is to bring the whole
man to the earth – with all the beautiful qualities
of woman and with all the courageous,
rebellious, adventurous qualities of man.
And they should all be part of one whole.

Mind is just like a tree: questions grow on the
tree like leaves. If you cut one leaf, the tree
will replace it with three leaves, at least.
That's how a gardener makes the tree thick,
the foliage big.

Mind is very productive as far as questions are
concerned. It manufactures only questions.
And each answer, mind will immediately change
into hundreds of questions. No answer
is going to stop the mind.

Thinking is of the mind.
Understanding is of the beyond.
So the first thing to be noted is that to attain to
understanding one has not to become a very
keen thinker. On the contrary, one has to
become a no-thinker. In the state of non-thinking
blossoms the flower of understanding.

Your thoughts have to understand one thing:
that you are not interested in them.
The moment you have made this point
you have attained a tremendous victory.
Just watch.
Don't say anything to the thoughts.
Don't judge. Don't condemn.
Don't tell them to move.
Let them do whatsoever they are doing, any
gymnastics let them do; you simply watch, enjoy.
It is just a beautiful film.
And you will be surprised: just watching,
a moment comes when thoughts are not there,
there is nothing to watch.

You have so much time – standing in a bus, sitting in a train, lying down on the bed. I see people playing cards, smoking cigars, going to the cinema hall. And you ask them, "Why are you doing all this?"

They say, "Killing time."

People have so much time that they are killing it! They don't know any other use for it.

Please, just those moments which you want to kill – save them for meditation. And I don't want any other change in your life. I am not asking much: simply don't kill time. And that time which you have been killing up to now...now let that time kill you!

The whole art of meditation is the art of remembering who you are.

The indications that you are on the right path are very simple: your tensions will start disappearing, you will become more and more cool, you will become more and more calm, you will find beauty in things which you have never, ever conceived could be beautiful.

The smallest things will start having tremendous significance. The whole world will become more and more mysterious every day; you will become less and less knowledgeable, more and more innocent – just like a child running after butterflies or collecting seashells on the beach.

You will feel life not as a problem but as a gift, as a blessing, as a benediction.

These indications will go on growing if you are on the right track. If you are on the wrong track, just the opposite will happen.

Remember, we are always in the hands of death, so don't postpone the essential.

Postpone the non-essential. The essential has to be done now.

Questions and quest are two different things.
Questions are simply curiosities.

Quest is a risk, is a pilgrimage, is a search.

A question is easily satisfied by any logical, rational answer. The quest is not satisfied by logical or rational answers; the quest is like thirst.

You can go on repeating that scientifically, H_2O means water, but that is not going to quench the thirst. It is an answer, and a perfectly right answer; if somebody is asking what water is, as a question, it is very simple to answer it.

But if somebody is asking about water because he is thirsty, then H_2O is not going to help. Then, only real water will do.

Listen perfectly.
Never bother about remembering, because that is a disturbance. Doing the two things together, then one starts taking notes – if not visibly, then inside the mind.

No, don't create disturbance, just listen. If something is true, your heart will simply absorb it. And the heart has no memory system. The memory system is in the head.

But whatever the heart absorbs will be changing your actions, will be changing your behavior, will be changing you. It will bring a transformation.

It will not bring you knowledge, it will bring you transformation. It will make you a new man.

You are not the container but the content. Discarding the container and discovering the content is the whole process of enlightenment.

Meditation starts taking you beyond time because it is going to take you beyond death.

You will be surprised that in Sanskrit there is only one word for both death and time. It is **kal**. **Kal** also means tomorrow – tomorrow there is only death and nothing else; life is today.

As you become peaceful... Your tensions are your weight. When the tensions are not there, you become weightless.

And the consciousness which is your reality has no time-space limitation.

Your body grows from childhood to youth to old age to death – these changes are happening only to the body. These are the changes of the furniture in the house...painting the house, changing its architecture. But the man who lives in the house – the master of the house – is unaffected by all these things.

Consciousness is the master.

Your body is only the house.

So the moment you enter meditation you have touched within yourself something of the universal – which has no age, which has no limitation either of time or space.

Take risks, be a gambler – what can you lose? We come with empty hands, we go with empty hands. There is nothing to lose.

It is a small life, given to you as a school.
Train yourself for all the pleasures.

You are not given everything by birth. You
are given by birth only the necessary things
for survival; everything else is given only as a
seed. If you are intentionally interested in
evolving your consciousness to its highest peak,
then it is up to you.

Nature provides only for survival – not life, not
joy, not silence, not ecstasy, not love. Nature can
manage itself with only lust – what is the need
for love? Why create complications?

Love you will have to find, consciousness you
will have to grow. You will have to become a
gardener of your own being – your being is your
garden.

You will have to change the meaning of love.
It is not something that you are trying to get
from the other. And this has been the whole
history of love – everybody is trying to get it from
the other, as much as possible. Both are trying to
get, and naturally nobody is getting anything.

Love is not something to get.
Love is something to give.
But you can give only when you have.

The experience of orgasm not only gives you the ultimate pleasure that the body is capable of, it also gives you the insight that this is not all. It opens a door. It makes you aware that you have been unnecessarily looking outside, your real treasure is within.

Meditation has been found by people who had deep orgasmic experiences. Meditation is a byproduct of orgasmic experience. There is no other way to find meditation. But orgasm brings you naturally into a state of meditation: time stops, thinking disappears, the ego is no more. You are pure energy. For the first time you understand: you are not the body and you are not the mind; you are something that transcends both – a conscious energy.

And once you enter into the realm of conscious energy, you start having the most beautiful experiences of life, the lightest, the most colorful, the most poetic, the most creative. They give you fulfillment and contentment on the one hand – as far as the body, the mind and the world are concerned.

On the other hand, they create a tremendous, divine discontentment. Because what you have experienced is great, but the very experience of it makes you certain, for no reason at all, that there must be greater experiences ahead. Before you knew anything about orgasm, you had never dreamed about it; now you know it. This is going to become an incentive to seek and search: Is there anything more juicy, more blissful, more psychedelic than any psychedelics can deliver to you?

This search led man toward meditation.

Moment to moment, we will see.
Why go on doing rehearsals?
When the moment comes, your consciousness
will face it and respond to it.

But people are preparing so much that almost
their whole lives are used up in preparations.

To have a personality is hypocrisy.
To be an individual is your birthright.

Meditation transforms.
It takes you to higher levels of
consciousness and changes your whole lifestyle.
It changes your reactions into responses, to such
an extent that it is unbelievable that the person
who would have reacted in the same situation
in anger is now acting with deep compassion,
with love – in the same situation.

Meditation is a state of being, arrived at
through understanding.

It is only in our sleep that we are separate.
The moment we are awake we are one.

If the man has the right to fulfill his dreams, the woman has also the same right to fulfill her dreams. And when you have decided to be together, now it becomes something of a sacred duty to be careful that you don't trample on the dreams of the other.

Nothing hurts more than when a dream is crushed, when a hope dies, when the future becomes dark, when all the great ideas that you have been thinking your life to be made of seem to be impossible because this woman, or this man, is continuously destroying your mood, destroying your peace, destroying your silence. And when these things are destroyed, you cannot be creative. You can only be destructive, you can only be violent.

Life has immense treasures, which remain unknown to people because they don't have time. Their whole time is engaged in some kind of fight with someone – the other. The other contains the whole world.

And the greatest calamity that happens is that when you are fighting with the other, you slowly slowly forget yourself. Your whole focus becomes the other, and when the focus becomes the other you are lost.

Escaping to the Himalayas is not going to help, because even in the Himalayas your mind will remain the same, just you will not have the opportunity to know it. And it is better to know the enemy than not to know it, because by knowing there is a possibility to change. Not knowing is very dangerous.

When a disease is diagnosed, it is half cured. When a disease is not diagnosed, then comes the real problem. Medicine is not the problem; diagnosis is the problem.

The most successful lovers in the world are those who never meet. They make the most romantic, beautiful stories – no quarrel, no nagging, no fighting. And they never come to find out that "This is not the woman made for me and I am not the man made for this woman" – they never come close enough to know this.

But unfortunately, most lovers get married.

That is the most unfortunate accident in life.

It is possible that you may have to change your lovers many times in life. There is no harm in it. In fact, by changing your lovers many times in life you will be enriched....

Love knows no jealousy, love knows no complaint.
Love is a deep understanding.

You love someone – that does not mean that the other should love you also. It is not a contract.

Try to understand the meaning of love.

And you will not be able to understand the meaning of love by your so-called love affairs.

Strangely enough, you will understand the meaning of love by going deep into meditation, by becoming more silent, more together, more at ease. You will start radiating a certain energy; you will become loving, and you will know the beautiful qualities of love.

There is no failure in life. It all depends how you take things. If you are desiring too much – you want to reach too high, and you cannot – then there is frustration and failure. But if you are not desiring anything and you are perfectly happy wherever you are, life is a moment-to-moment victory.

Words become realities to people. Always remember to use words with right connotations.

As you become more sensitive, life becomes bigger. It is not a small pond, it becomes oceanic. It is not confined to you and your wife and your children – it is not confined at all. This whole existence becomes your family; and unless the whole existence is your family you have not known what life is – because no man is an island; we are all connected.

We are a vast continent, joined in millions of ways. And if our hearts are not full of love for the whole, in the same proportion our life is cut short.

Meditation will bring you sensitivity, a great sense of belonging to the world. It is our world – the stars are ours, and we are not foreigners here. We belong intrinsically to existence.

We are part of it, we are **heart** of it.

Judgment is an ugly phenomenon. Rise in your own being – higher. Don't destroy that opportunity by judging other people as lower. You are doing immense harm to yourself, not to anybody else.

Any question asked by any human being is going to be a question of all human beings, whether you are aware of it or not. You may be unconscious of it; perhaps it is not the right time for you, perhaps you may ask a year later. Perhaps you have repressed the question so deeply that you have become completely oblivious to whether it exists in you or not.

But let me repeat: There is not a single question which is not yours too.

My answers are not answers, in fact. My answers are killers – they simply kill the question, they take away the question, they don't give you any answer to hold on to.

And that is the difference between a teacher and a master: the teacher gives you answers so that you can hold those answers and remain ignorant – beautifully decorated on the surface, libraries full of answers, but underneath, below the surface, an abysmal ignorance.

The master simply kills your questions.

He does not give you an answer, he takes away the question.

If all your questions can be taken away....

Listen carefully to what I am saying:

If all your questions can be taken away, your ignorance is bound to disappear, and what remains is innocence.

And innocence is a light unto itself.

Look – life is not a difficult matter. It becomes a problem when your life wants to go one way and your mind drags you in another, and you are in a conflict, torn apart. You can go to neither side, because half of you is trying to go in another direction.

Life becomes absolutely simple once you start functioning from something that is higher than your mind.

In the beginning, for any seeker, the whole search is to find a space above the mind.

Once you have found a small space above the mind, all dualism disappears, all tensions, all anxieties disappear. And strangely enough, the mind which was never in your control, suddenly surrenders itself to you.

Mind as a master is a disaster.

Mind as a servant is a beautiful gift of nature. You just have to find the master – and it is not very far away, it is just above the mind.

Only one step.

You get to the heart and it is so beautiful, so lovely, one would like to remain.
There is no point in going anywhere anymore, it seems everything is achieved.

But you will have to leave it.

And the departure is a little painful, but the pain will be forgotten immediately – because more and more blissfulness will be showering on you. And soon you will learn this: that there is no need to feel pain when you depart from one overnight stay. You become accustomed, you know that the journey is endless. And the treasure becomes more and more, you are not a loser. Stopping anywhere will be a loss.

So there is no stop, no full-stop... not even a semicolon.

You will have to learn to enjoy even the sweet pain of departing from beautiful spaces to more beautiful spaces.

Ignorance is the beginning of wisdom. Rightly understood, it is not something negative. It is simply a tabula rasa, a clean slate. Nothing is written on it. You have to write your own holy Bible, holy Koran, holy Gita, you have to give birth.

Ignorance is a womb.

It contains the quest for truth – and if you don't fall victim to knowledgeability, ignorance is the right beginning.

To know absolutely that "I do not know" is the first step of wisdom. You have known something of tremendous value: you have known your innocence.

The real moments of love remain unspoken. When you are really feeling love, that very feeling creates around you a certain radiance that says everything that you cannot say, that can never be said.

Each love affair is dangerous, because one has to lose oneself. From a distance it is perfectly good. Lovers think of so many things in their minds that they are going to say when they meet their beloved, their lover. But when they meet they suddenly become dumb. Just the closeness creates a change – the chattering mind is no more chattering, and there is a fear. If love is authentic there is bound to be fear.

If your love is not the ordinary, biological instinctive love, if it is not part of your ego, if it is not a power trip to dominate someone – if your love is just a pure joy, rejoicing in the being of the other for no reason at all, a sheer joy – awareness will follow this pure love just like a shadow. You need not worry about awareness.

There are only two ways: either you become aware, then love follows as a shadow; or you become so loving that awareness comes on its own accord. They are two sides of the same coin. You need not bother about the other side; just keep one side, the other side cannot escape. The other side is bound to come.

Mind cannot exist without problems; problems are its nourishment. Conflict, fight, disharmony – and the mind is perfectly at ease and at home.

Silence, harmony – and the mind starts becoming afraid, because harmony, silence and peace are nothing but death to the mind.

If you cannot laugh, you will miss many things in life, you will miss many mysteries.
Your laughter makes you a small innocent child, your laughter joins you with existence – with the roaring ocean, with the stars and the silence.

My own approach is very simple:
You have to be alert not to allow the heart to start overpowering your reason, just as you have to be alert that your reason does not overpower your heart. Their functions are separate. Reason should function in the world of objects, and heart should function in the world of human consciousness. And the moment they overlap, there is going to be a certain kind of mess.

When you are angry, have you observed? – your body takes a certain posture. In anger you cannot keep your hands open; in anger – the fist. In anger you cannot smile – or can you?

With a certain emotion, the body has to follow a certain posture.

Just small things are deeply related inside.

The ego is only an absence of awareness.
The room is full of darkness; you want the
darkness to leave the room. You can do
everything in your power – push it out, beat
it out – but you are not going to succeed.
Strangely enough, you will be defeated by
something which does not exist. Exhausted, your
mind will say the darkness is so powerful that it is
not within your capacity to dispel it, to expel it.
But that conclusion is not right; it is German, but
it is not right.

Just a small candle has to be brought in.

You don't have to expel the darkness. You
don't have to fight with it – that is sheer stupidity.
Just bring in a small candle, and the darkness is
not found anymore. Not that it goes out – it
cannot go out, because in the first place it does
not exist. Neither was it in, nor does it go out.

The light comes in, the light goes out; it has
positive existence. You can light a candle and
there is no darkness; you can blow out the
candle and there is darkness. To do anything
with darkness, you will have to do something
with light – very strange, very illogical, but what
can you do? Such is the nature of things.

My love is just like the light – it is neither more for somebody nor less for somebody. But still, for the blind man it will not exist. For the one who cannot see properly, it will be dim. And for one who can see with a clarity it will have a different intensity.

It is the same light, but it will depend how much you can receive.

If you are totally open, you can receive it all.

You should not be desirous of anything. The moment you come to the state of desirelessness, then existence uses you in whatever way is needed: as a mystic, as a master, as a singer, as a dancer, as a flute player – or just as nobody; but everything is a benediction.

That which comes to you from existence without your desiring it is always the greatest ecstasy there is.

Meditation is simply an understanding. It is not a question of sitting silently, it is not a question of chanting a mantra. It is a question of understanding the subtle workings of the mind.

As you understand those workings of the mind a great awareness arises in you which is not *of* the mind. That awareness arises in your being, in your soul, in your consciousness.

At the age of fourteen, one is sexually mature – mind starts functioning in a totally different way; the body starts functioning in a totally different way. Fourteen is the biological age for man: he is now able to produce children. As far as biology is concerned, man has come of age.

That's why the psychological age of humanity remains at fourteen: because now biology takes no interest in your psychological development unless you yourself are interested. Nature has brought you up to that point for its own purposes, for reproduction; its work is done. It is now only up to you if you want to be a seeker, to grow psychologically, to grow in your awareness. If you want a spiritual experience then everything is left to you; now it is up to you, nature has ended its work.

And because nature has stopped, 99.9 percent of people stop with nature. They were not evolving, it was the push of nature that brought them up to the age of fourteen.

The story of pleasures – physical, biological, psychological – begins at fourteen, and if nobody interferes and you are allowed to experience them, at the age of forty-two you will be naturally free of all kinds of bondages. It does not mean that you will escape from the world. It simply means that your wife will become your friend, your husband will become your friend. You will both understand that it was a certain biological force, which is spent, and now there is no need to harass each other unnecessarily. Now it is better, rather than harassing, to sit in meditation.

And I am saying this: if everything goes naturally, then reaching age forty-two will automatically bring a tremendous change in your life. You will remain in the world but absolutely unattached. This is true renunciation – no obsession, nothing repressed. The heart is clean, there is no garbage inside.

Hate is destructive, self-destructive. Love is tremendous respect for oneself. You may hate anything, anybody; you may hate hate itself, but in every way you will find yourself low-energy. Hate sucks your energy, leaves you empty, spent.

Love fills you with energy, with overflowing energy – not only healing you, but creating an aura around you in which others may be healed.

It is not a question of religion – that hate is bad or immoral. It is a question of intelligence: hate is stupid and love is intelligent.

Have you seen two dogs fighting? Most probably they will bark at each other, jump at each other, and you will see that there is going to be a bloody fight – but nothing happens. They judge and see who is stronger, and once it is accepted by both that one is stronger than the other, there is no need to fight. Then one dog simply puts his tail down, gives the signal: "Stop it. You are the winner, I am the defeated, and we can still be good friends."

Dogs are more intelligent than politicians.

When I criticize the politician, it is not the politician outside you, it is the politician within you.

The outer politician is only a manifestation, a collective manifestation of your inner politicians. You are all searching in some way or other to have more, to possess more, to be powerful, to be dominant, to be special: V.V.I.P – a V.I.P. is no longer enough.

When I criticize the politicians I am criticizing the political structure of your mind....

I have to criticize the politicians because they are what you would like to be. Presidents, prime ministers, governors, ambassadors – that's what you would like to be, but it is only a seed in you. And in the seed you cannot see all the flowers and all the colors. When I criticize the politicians I am criticizing you as if your politician had come into power.

Compromise simply means you are on uncertain ground. Rather than compromising, find grounding, roots, individuality. Find a sincerity of feeling, the support of your heart. Then whatever the consequence it does not matter.

Unless you create, you are going to remain self-destructive. It is the same energy. You have the energy, you are a dynamo of energy, continuously being created from the cosmos. What will you do with it? If you don't create you are going to be destructive, you are going to destroy.

You come into the world without anything, so one thing is certain: nothing belongs to you. You come absolutely naked, but with illusions. That's why every child is born with closed hands, fists, believing that he is bringing treasures – and those fists are just empty. And everybody dies with open hands. Try to die with fists – nobody has been successful up to now. Or try to be born with open hands – nobody has been successful in that, either.

The child is born with fists, with illusions that he is bringing treasures into the world, but there is nothing in the fist. Nothing belongs to you, so what insecurity are you worried about? Nothing can be stolen, nothing can be taken away from you.

Everything that you are using belongs to the world. And one day, you have to leave everything here. You will not be able to take anything with you.

Consciousness is not your body, nor your mind, nor your heart. So when a person dies, he dies for you, not for himself. For himself he simply changes the house, perhaps moves into a better apartment. But because the old apartment is left, and you are searching for him in the old apartment and you don't find him there, you think the poor guy is dead. All that you should say is, "The poor guy escaped ! Now where he has gone, we don't know."

The dialectics of life is that the people who make great effort for enlightenment will not achieve by their effort. One day they will have to give it all up, and in that moment of relaxation something opens up – you are not the doer, something happens to you.

And the same is true about scientific discoveries – the law is the same. A scientist works for years on a certain project, and then one day he has done everything that he could possibly think of; he drops the whole idea. And suddenly a window opens, and what he was searching for with such great effort is made available to him without any effort at all.

In fact, there are deep reasons in it: whenever you are making effort you become tense; when you are tense, your mind becomes narrow. And you are so ambitious, so desirous, so much in a hurry to get something, that you are almost a chaos.

And to know anything – either scientific or religious – you need to be a silent, peaceful awareness, not doing anything, not even desiring anything, not even looking for anything.

But all the time before, when you have been looking and not finding, has created a certain seed in you. In this relaxed moment, that seed starts becoming a sprout.

There is no need to know where you are going.
There is no need to know why you are going.

All that is needed to be known is that you are going joyously, because if you are going joyously you cannot go wrong.

Life is beautiful because there is so much which cannot be explained. It would have been a disaster if life consisted only of things which can be explained.

Just think for a moment:

If everything could be explained, then there would be no mystery, then there would be no poetry, then there would be no secret. Then everything would be utterly flat and boring.

Life is not a boredom because there are dimensions in it that you can go on exploring, yet you can never come to explanations. You can experience much, yet even that which you have experienced cannot be translated into words.

Life is not just what it seems. It is tremendously much more, it is incalculably much more.

But you will have to turn your face towards yourself.

Each individual has to explore in his own way.

There is no superhighway with milestones telling you how far you are from the goal. In the spiritual exploration, you have to walk and create your path by your walking; there is no ready-made path such that you have simply to walk on it.

And my feeling is that this is tremendously blissful and ecstatic. You are not like railway trains. Running on rails you cannot run into the jungles, into the mountains, anywhere you like. The railway train is a prisoner.

But a river is not a prisoner. It also travels long. It may be coming thousands of miles, from the Himalayas, and it reaches finally to the ocean – with no map, with no guidelines, with no guides, and nobody on the way of whom the river can inquire, "Which way am I to go now?"…because each step is a crossroads.

But strangely enough, every river reaches to the ocean with great freedom, finding its own path.

Everybody, as he is, is needed.
And he is needed as he is.
That's why you are born in a certain way.
    Don't try to go astray from your nature.

Meditation is just
a courage to be silent
and alone.

Birth happens to you, youth happens to you, love happens to you, old age happens to you, death happens to you – whatever is essential happens to you and whatever is non-essential is left for you to do.

So don't waste your whole life in the non-essential.

That non-essential is also needed, but remember that the essential has not to be forgotten.

And you have not to do anything for it;
you have just to be receptive, open, vulnerable,
available, so that if the call comes from the
beyond you will be ready to say with your
full heart,
   "Yes, I am coming."

Indifference to the mind is meditation. Mind is the problem. When there is no mind, then there is peace, so how can there be peace of mind?

And any "peace of mind" is only fallacious; it simply means the noise has slowed down to such a point that you think it is silence. And you don't have anything to compare it with.

Enlightenment is not caused by effort. By effort, relaxation is caused. You have done so much that you simply give up.

But without doing it, you cannot give up.

Birth is only an opportunity. Either you can learn to live a beautiful life or you can just drag yourself towards the graveyard. It is up to you. There are people for whom life is a drag, and there are people for whom even death is a dance.

I want to say to you that if you make your life an art, your death will be the culmination of the art – the highest peak, a beauty in itself.

The West has created instant coffee, but the West does not know how to sip it. Enlightenment is nothing but the right, meditative way of drinking coffee.

Existence is hilarious!
If you just have eyes to see the hilarious points you will be surprised: in life there is no place to be serious. Everybody is slipping on banana peels – you just need an insight to see.

The functioning of the heart and the mind are totally different; not only different but diametrically opposite. The mind creates philosophies, theologies, ideologies – they are all questions that don't have any answer. The heart simply waits. At the right moment, the answer blossoms by itself.

The heart has no question, yet it receives the answer.

The mind has a thousand and one questions, yet it has never received any answer because it does not know how to receive.

Man's misery is that he is trying to do the impossible; he is trying to force the heart to serve the mind, which is impossible. This is your chaos, this is your mess.

Sadness has its own beauty.
It has tremendous depth, it has its own calmness, quietness, softness. It is a beautiful experience. So don't try to avoid it. If you avoid it, you are avoiding the door to silence.

Enjoy it, receive it with open hands, embrace it. The more you are welcoming, the sooner sadness will start changing into silence.

And silence, slowly slowly, becomes a music without sound.

There is a very delicate, fine line between ignorance and innocence. A child is ignorant, not innocent. And when you are reborn in a spiritual way you become again like a child. Remember, I am saying "like a child." I am not saying you become a child – you become **like** a child, innocent.

The division between ignorance and innocence is so fine, but the ignorant person is always trying not to be ignorant – these are the symptoms – he is trying to become knowledgeable. The innocent person is trying to be more innocent. If any knowledge has remained somewhere hanging around him, he is trying to throw it away. He wants to be completely clean.

Just ignore, just be aloof, just let the mind to whatever it wants to do. When the mind feels unwelcomed, when the mind sees that you are no more interested in it, that it is pointless to go on shouting, you are not even hearing it; that you are not even curious about what is going on in the mind – it stops.

I want you to accept yourself as you are. That's how existence wanted you to be. You have not created yourself; naturally the whole responsibility goes to existence, and there must be a need for a person like you – otherwise, you would not exist.

Existence needs you as you are.

The word 'sin' in its roots means forgetfulness. It has nothing to do with sin as we have come to understand it.

To forget yourself is the only sin.

And to remember yourself is the only virtue.

Life is a beautiful experiment to solve problems. The more problems you solve, the more intelligent you become.

Escaping is not the way.

If you want life, abundant life,
then be ready to die.
Dying each moment so that each moment you
are reborn is the whole secret of all religion.

It is said that even before a river falls into the ocean, it trembles with fear. It looks back at the whole journey, the peaks of the mountains, the long winding path through the forests, through the people, and it sees in front of it such a vast ocean that entering into it is nothing but disappearing forever. But there is no other way.

The river cannot go back.

Neither can you go back.

Going back is impossible in existence; you can only go forward. The river has to take the risk and go into the ocean. And only when it enters the ocean will the fear disappear, because only then will the river know that it is not disappearing into the ocean, rather it is becoming the ocean.

It is a disappearance from one side and it is a tremendous resurrection on the other side.

The master takes away only things which you don't have, but you think you have. And he goes on giving you things which you have, but you have forgotten completely that they are your intrinsic nature.

All that you know is this small life, and in this small life you know two things: the misery and the pain of life, and ways and methods of forgetting that misery and pain. That you call your amusement, entertainment – going to a movie, to a circus. These are your ways to forget your life. There, you become engaged for two or three hours in a different world.

The enlightened person is certainly difficult for you to conceive of….

When you think about enlightenment, the problem is that you don't understand that the man who is enlightened is no more an ego. You can insult him but you cannot hurt him; you can abuse him, you can condemn him, and there will be no change in his being.

Even if you kill him he will remain the same.

It is difficult for you to understand how an enlightened man can remain without going to circuses, movies…and all kinds of stupidities are there.

But so few enlightened people have existed that not much is known about them. And much is such that unless you experience it, you cannot understand it.

For the enlightened person, everything that is going on around him is a circus. There is no need for him to purchase a ticket – his problem is how to get out of the circus! He does not want to go to the movie, he wants to get out!

It is certain that in my earlier teachings to you, enlightenment appeared to be much easier. It had to, because I did not want you to freak out.

Now I can trust that even if I say the truth you are not going to escape:

Enlightenment is not easy.

The moment you open your door, immediately the fragrance of the flowers enters without making any noise. The sun rays enter. A cool breeze comes in. You have opened the door to the whole universe.

To be available to the master is just an excuse. You will be afraid to be open to the whole universe – it will be too much. The master convinces you that there is no need to open all the doors and all the windows, "Just open a small window – a special window for me."

But once you open even a small window, the whole sky enters in.

My whole love and respect is for the person who accepts himself totally, as he is. He has courage. He has courage to face the whole pressure of the society which is bent upon splitting him into divisions – into good and bad, into saint and sinner. He is really a brave, courageous being who stands against the whole history of man, of morality, and declares to the skies his reality, whatever it is.

And at least with the master, the disciple has to be absolutely clean and clear so the master can start working with your reality, not with your phoniness. Because everything done with your phoniness is a sheer wastage.

Only the real you is capable of growing, of coming to a flowering.

146

If you want to change the world,
don't start by changing the world –
that is the wrong way humanity has followed
up to now: Change the society, change the
economic structure, change this, change that,
but don't change the individual.

That's why all revolutions have failed.
Only one revolution can succeed,
which has not been tried up to now –
and that is the revolution of the individual.

You change yourself.

Be alert not to contribute anything
that makes the world a hell.
And remember to contribute
to the world something
that makes it a paradise.

This is the whole secret
of a religious man.
And if every individual starts doing it,
there will be a revolution
without any bloodshed.

The phenomenon of weeping is mysterious. It does not mean that you are sad, not necessarily. It is not necessarily against celebrating, against cheerfulness, against laughing; no.

The tears have a very strange function: whenever something in your heart is so much that it cannot be expressed by normal means, tears are an emergency method. So they may mean anything.

You may be very happy, so happy that laughing will look stupid but tears will look perfectly right. Your tears will show that your happiness is not an ordinary happiness – it is so deep that only tears can express it; it is so extraordinarily deep that an emergency method is used.

Two friends meeting after many days, many years, may not feel like talking; talking may look too profane. They may like just to hug each other and weep on each other's shoulders. They are saying many many things…many many memories, many many questions; unresolved moments of experience, of love. Tears will help to unburden them.

Remember, if you feel me in your heart, then I am coming with you. Wherever you go, I am coming with you – and without a ticket, because they have not yet found a way to know whether a person is traveling with someone hiding in his heart.

Music is born out of deep experiences of meditation; it is a dimension of meditation. By meditating you may be able to be touched by music, but the reverse is also true: If you are totally absorbed in music, your heart will be touched not only by music but by meditation too.

Music is sound. Meditation is soundlessness. The highest music is where the sound does not destroy the soundless moments in between. As the musician becomes more and more refined, he can manage to create sound and between two sounds he can give you an experience of soundlessness.

That soundlessness touches the heart.

The mind is a habit.
Even if there are moments when the heart is singing and the whole being is full of joy, the mind cannot leave its old habits.

It will certainly ask what is happening.

Can't you allow things to happen without asking why? what?

Do you understand why we ask such questions?

The mind asks these questions because it wants to control your lifestyle, it wants to know everything that is going on. Nothing should happen which is beyond it; everything should be in its control.

The mind is a great controller. And if everything remains in its control, it will be a tragedy because nothing great can happen to you.

Everything that is great, magnificent, is beyond mind.

And mind can never get the answer why, what, how.

You have to learn one thing: that it is not necessary to satisfy the mind about every experience.

Experiences of the heart, experiences of the being, experiences of the transcendental should not be made a point of inquiry. You should not ask why, you should enjoy them.

You should not ask what is happening, because if you insist on these questions the happening will stop. These questions are not your friends.

Let the mind ask questions only when something is going wrong. You are sick, you have a headache, your stomach has cramps – let the mind ask; that is the right realm for the mind.

Enlightenment has nothing to do with mind; it has something to do with awareness **of** the mind. It does not go into the details of the mind, what it consists of, how it functions, all its mechanics. Awareness is simply disidentification with the mind; mind is left behind as a mechanism.

The moment the mind is completely left behind and there is only pure awareness, just a luminosity, it is enlightenment.

I accept you as you are, but that does not
mean that I want you to remain as you are.
I love you as you are, but I love you because you
have so much potential in you, such a great
possibility of growth, that with just a little effort
you can become a light unto yourself.

Whatever you are, enjoy it. But there is much
more, so don't stop at it.

You are on the first rung of the ladder – it is
perfectly good, because without being on the
first rung, how can you be on the second and
how can you be on the final, the ultimate?

Nobody is a sinner.

Yes, there are people who commit mistakes,
but nobody is a sinner. And everybody has a
right to commit mistakes – because that is the
only way to learn. And everybody has to stumble
in the dark. That is nothing special to you;
everybody falls once in a while, and it is a good
training.

To me, whatever existence makes available to
you is for your good. Just use it, and keep your
eyes on the faraway stars – they belong to you.

However far they are, they are not beyond
your reach.

It is good and fortunate that nothing satisfies you completely and entirely. That means you don't become stagnant, that means you have to keep moving.

Slowly slowly, you will understand that there is no home, that movement itself is the home; that there is no end to the pilgrimage but the pilgrimage itself is the end.

It is very difficult to understand because we are accustomed to a certain logic: if we want to go somewhere, going is always just a means, reaching somewhere is the end.

But as far as the universal life is concerned, there cannot be a place where you can say, "I have come and now there is nothing further."

It is inconceivable that you will find a place which will be the end and there will be a fence and a board saying, "Here ends the world."

And even if you can find such a place, I would like you to jump the fence – because there must be something beyond the fence. The fence cannot just stand by itself, there must be something beyond it. Somebody is playing a joke by putting up a board – "Here ends the world" – and fixing a fence there. Don't be deceived.

NOTHING
is my sword.
It is so thin you cannot see it.
    And the work is certainly so delicate,
it cannot be done with crude instruments.
    Do you see the sword of 'nothing' in my
hands?
    It is there.

People have been told such nonsense for centuries – as if spirituality is a kind of geography, so that maps are given to you, guidelines are provided to you: Follow the right guidelines and you will reach the goal.

Alas, things are not so cheap. There are no maps in existence; no solid guidelines either, because each individual is so unique that what may be a guideline for one may prove a distraction for another; what may be medicine to one may prove poison to another.

Individuals are so different....

No general guidelines can be provided.

I say many things to you without saying them.
I simply create the atmosphere by saying many
other things in which you can hear the unsaid.

Because there are a few things which can
only be whispered, not shouted. And there are
a few things which cannot even be whispered
but only indicated indirectly; only then
are they beautiful.

In this whole society, as an intelligent and alert
person, you are bound to be surprised:
Why do things go on happening the way they
should not?

Wars are not needed, riots are not needed,
bloodshed is not needed, nuclear weapons are
not needed. Half of the earth is dying from
starvation and you are preparing more
destructive weapons. It is simply insane.

But the trouble is that all these insane
people have the same interest. The presidents
and the prime ministers of all the nations, all
the countries, have the same interest. If nations
disappear, they will disappear – what about
their power trip?

I want you to be absolutely selfish so that you
can blossom in your full glory. Your blossoming
will trigger blossomings in others, your flame will
bring light, life and fire to many.

But this has not to be done directly. It is not
your business. It is simply the impact of your
transformed life.

157

It seems to be something in the very nature of life, that the people who are going to be decisive about human consciousness will always come ahead of their time – because it takes one hundred years, two hundred years for people to understand them. If they come in their own time, then by the time people have understood them, they will be out of date. They have to be ahead of their time so that by the time human mind, human consciousness reaches the point where they can be understood, their message will be available.

Don't ask what is happening.
Let it happen, and see.
What I am saying is nothing; what will happen
will be a thousandfold more.

Remember that every experience on the path, in the beginning is a great shock. Your very roots are shaken. Whatever you have believed to be true is no longer true. Whatever you have been thinking of as real is dream stuff, and whatever you have never thought about seems to be the ultimate reality. The change is so much and so quick that it is natural for human beings to be afraid. But the fear is only because you are ignorant of the experience.

A man is dead if he has no challenge in his life. It is the challenge that proves you are alive – just breathing and temperature and heartbeats do not prove that you are alive, they only prove that the body is still alive. Whether you are alive or not is a different question.

You are alive when faraway stars challenge you for a pilgrimage. Unknown realities, unheard-of truths, unexperienced beauties…when they become your real world you have a life with joy and with dance and with song.

The way of love is the way of no-expectation. Love exists only when there is a total acceptance and no desire to change anything.

In life, everything that is important only **happens**. Things that you have to **do** are unimportant things – utilitarian, needed, but not essential to your being.

One of the greatest things to learn on the path is to discriminate between these two different worlds: the world of doing and the world of happening. They are all mixed up in your minds.

There are things that can only be done – you cannot just wait for existence to do them for you. And there are things that, whatever you do, you are going to fail. Only in your utter failure, when you give up, they happen. They happen from the beyond.

A whole man is available to both, to doing and to happening. But remember: whatever you do is momentary, and whatever you do is lower than you, it cannot be higher than you. Action cannot be higher than the doer.

And in **happening** whatsoever happens is higher than you; it comes upon you from above. It showers on you as if it is a rain of flowers, blessings, benediction.

So if a man can sort out that which is "doing" and that which is "happening" his life will have a clarity, a great intelligence, and a tremendous possibility of fulfillment.

With me, the trouble is that I am absolutely honest.

To provoke people, you have to be offensive. To create a new ground for a new humanity, you have to destroy much of the past – and you cannot be other than hard.

If I simply talk about abstract concepts which are not any danger to the existing society, to the vested interests, I will be respected – the same people who are enemies now will start talking about me as a great saint – but I will not be of any help to those who are really thirsty.

So I am not worried about all of humanity.

My concern is that I must reach each door and knock at least once.

If somebody can understand, he should not miss.

If somebody cannot understand, there is no harm – he was not going to understand anyway.

So everything that is being done is well planned and deliberate. It is not accidental.

The greatest work for sannyasins is to keep the message pure, unpolluted by you or by others – and wait.

The future is bound to be more receptive, more welcoming. We may not be here but we can manage to change the consciousness for centuries to come. And my interest is not only in this humanity, my interest is in humanity as such.

Keep the message pure, twenty-four carat gold. And soon those people will be coming for whom you have made a temple – although it is sad when you are making the temple; nobody comes. And when people start coming, you will not be here.

But one has to understand one thing: we are part of a flowing river of consciousness. You may not be here in this form, you may be here in another form….

But keep it in mind never to ask that I should be more acceptable, more respectable, more in agreement with the masses. I cannot be. And it is not stubbornness on my part. It is just that truth cannot compromise. It has never done it; it would be the greatest sin.

Just imagine a world where people are meditative.

It will be a simple world, but it will be tremendously beautiful. It will be silent. It will not have crimes, it will not have courts, it will not have any kind of politics.

It will be a loving brotherhood, a vast commune of people who are absolutely satisfied with themselves, utterly contented with themselves. Even Alexander the Great cannot give them a gift.

True celebration should come from your life, in your life. And true celebration cannot be according to the calendar, that on the first of November you will celebrate. Strange, the whole year you are miserable and on the first of November suddenly you come out of misery, dancing. Either the misery was false or the first of November is false; both cannot be true. And once the first of November is gone, you are back in your dark hole, everybody in his misery, everybody in his anxiety.

Life should be a continuous celebration, a festival of lights the whole year round.

My function is simply that of a reminder. I want just to be a mirror to you so that you can see your original face. And if you can see a buddha in me, there is no difficulty in seeing the buddha in you too – maybe a little lazy, a little sleepy, a little gone off the track.

But a buddha is a buddha.

It does not matter whether his nuts and bolts are a little loose, we will fix them.

One's buddhahood is one's essential nature.

I don't want you to worship buddhas, I want you to become buddhas. That is the only right worship.

If you love, become it.

Life is a beautiful journey if it is a process of constant learning, exploration. Then it is excitement every moment, because every moment you are opening a new door, every moment you are coming in contact with a new mystery.

I love the truth – I have found it.
I have loved you – I have found you also. Now my only remaining work is to somehow turn your eyes towards the truth. Once that happens, then there is no need for me to be here.

But I am not a serious man, I can still be here. So you don't be worried; most probably I will be here.

Just concentrate your whole energy on meditation. Become silent, watch your thoughts moving on the screen of the mind. Just by watching they will disappear one day.

Don't be in a hurry.

You cannot do anything except watch and wait.

Remember these two words: **watch** and **wait**.
Whenever the time is ripe, your watchfulness is perfect, thoughts will disappear – and their disappearance means the opening of the whole existence.

This is what I call meditation.

The whole existence is a great verb, not a noun – not a stone, but a flower. And there is no end anywhere, because there has never been any beginning. The very idea of beginning and end is just our mind projection. Otherwise, we are always in the middle – never at the beginning, never at the end, always in the middle – and we will remain always in the middle.

I don't have a single principle for you to follow; just a simple understanding that it is your life – enjoy it, allow it to sing a song in you, allow it to become a dance in you. You have nothing else to do but simply to be available.

And flowers are going to shower on you.

When mind is silent, time disappears because mind is time.

Love is such a delicate flower that you cannot force it to be permanent. You can have plastic flowers; that's what people have – marriage, the family, the children, the relatives, everything is plastic. Plastic has one very spiritual thing: it is permanent!

Real love is as uncertain as your life is uncertain. You cannot say that you will be here tomorrow. You cannot even say that you are going to survive the next moment. Your life is continuously changing – from childhood to youth, to middle age, to old age, to death, it goes on changing.

Real love will also change.

I am not a hard taskmaster. First I create a beautiful dream, and then slowly slowly I take you out of it.

Now you are out of the dream, so the second problem arises – where is the path? In fact, it is my doing. While you were asleep I was talking about the path…"the path, the mystic path…" to wake you up. Now you are awake, so you are asking, "Where is the path?"

There is no path.

It was just a device to wake you up.

Beyond enlightenment is only beyondness. Enlightenment is the last host. Beyond it, all boundaries disappear, all experiences disappear.

Experience comes to its utmost in enlightenment; it is the very peak of all that is beautiful, of all that is immortal, of all that is blissful – but it is an experience.

Beyond enlightenment there is no experience at all, because the experiencer has disappeared.

Enlightenment is not only the peak of experience, it is also the finest definition of your being. Beyond it, there is only nothingness; you will not come again to a point which has to be transcended.

Experience, the experiencer, enlightenment – all have been left behind. You are part of the tremendous nothingness that is infinite.

The whole function of the master is to push you the same way a mother bird pushes a small bird, a new bird who has never opened his wings into the sky. Naturally he is afraid – a vast sky. He has lived in a small cozy nest, safe and secure, the mother has been taking care – and now she wants him to take a jump and fly. One day she pushes him. And the moment he is pushed out of the nest – for a moment it feels as if he is going to fall down on the earth, but before he falls on the earth his wings open and the whole sky is his.

And there are skies beyond skies.

I will not say to you that the home is everywhere – although it is true. I will say there is no home.

If you can continue your pilgrimage with this sincerity – that there is no home and there is no place you are going to, that just the going is in itself the beauty, the joy, the blissfulness, everything…the going itself – then it will also be true that wherever you are, it is home. But people are very cunning, even cunning with themselves. They have misused all truths, they have managed to give them meanings which support their own ideas. If I say, "Everywhere is home," then they will relax wherever they are, then there is no need.

So I say: there is no home, and the journey has to be continued. It has to be a dance. Take your guitars and go on, and never stop anywhere.

That does not mean that you cannot rest for a while. There are caravanserais, but no homes – stay over for the night, but in the morning we have to go. This ongoing process is what life is.

M ovement is life, change is life. Stay for a while if you feel tired, but stay only to regain enough energy so that tomorrow morning you can move again. The home **is** everywhere – but that home is just a caravanserai.

I have to work on two levels: one is the level where you live, where you are, and one is the level where I am and I want you also to be.

From the top of a hill I have to come into the valley where you are; otherwise you don't listen, you won't believe the sunlit top. I have to take your hand in my hand and persuade you – and on the way, tell stories which are not true!

But they keep you engaged, and you don't create any trouble in walking. You go on, engaged with the story. And when you have reached the hilltop, you will know why I was telling long stories, and you will feel grateful that I told those stories; otherwise you would not have been able to travel that long, that far uphill.

It is something to be remembered: all the masters of the world have been telling stories, parables – why? The truth can be simply said, there is no need to give you so many stories. But the night is long, and you have to be kept awake; without stories you are going to fall asleep.

Till the morning comes there is an absolute necessity to keep you engaged, and the stories the masters have been telling are the most intriguing things possible.

The truth cannot be said, but you can be led to the point from where you can see it. Now, the question is how to lead you to the point from where you can see it.

Whatever I am doing is to help you to evolve towards more peace, more silence, more love, more compassion – very simple qualities.

I am not asking you to follow great disciplines – stand on your head for twelve hours a day, or don't eat food for twenty-one days every year. I am not asking any austerities of you. I am simply asking you to rejoice in small things. Whatever you are eating, eat with joy; whoever your friends are, rejoice in their friendship. Whatever life has given to you, never complain. It is always more than you deserve.

Always be grateful.

And if you can learn the simple fact of gratefulness, your evolution will happen on its own accord.

Enlightenment happens when you have forgotten all about it. Don't even look out of the corner of your eye, just in case enlightenment is coming and you will miss it.

Forget all about it.

You just enjoy your simple life.

And everything is so beautiful – why create unnecessary anxiety and anguish for yourself? Strange problems of spirituality…those things are not something you can do anything about.

If you can make your ordinary life a thing of beauty and art, all that you had always desired will start happening on its own accord.

There is no end, because every end will be
death. And life knows no death; it goes
on and on and on.

So this is simply a preparation; it is always a
preparation for a new journey.

You can have a little rest, but remember:

It is just an overnight stay in a caravanserai.

In the morning we have to go,
so rest well, be ready.

As the sun rises, our journey starts again.

Life is from eternity to eternity.

The quotations used in More Gold Nuggets are from discourses given in Bombay, India, from August to December, 1986.The entire discourses are published in the following books by Osho Rajneesh:

The Rajneesh Upanishad

Beyond Enlightenment

Sermons in Stones

Worldwide Distribution Centers for the Works of Osho Rajneesh

Books by Osho Rajneesh are available in many languages throughout the world. His discourses have been recorded live on audiotape and videotape. There are many recordings of Rajneesh meditation music and celebration music played in His presence, as well as beautiful photographs of Osho Rajneesh. For further information contact one of the distribution centers below:

EUROPE

Belgium
Indu
Rajneesh Meditation Center
Coebergerstr. 40
2018 Antwerpen
Tel.   3/237 2037
Fax   3/216 9871

Denmark
Anwar Distribution
Carl Johansgade 8, 5
2100 Copenhagen
Tel. 01/420 218
Fax 01/147 348

Finland
Unio Mystica Shop
for Meditative Books & Tapes
Albertinkatu 10
P.O. Box 186
00121 Helsinki
Tel.   3580/665 811

Italy
Rajneesh Services
Corporation
Via XX Settembre 12
28041 Arona (NO)
Tel.   02/839 2194
(Milan office)
Fax   02/832 3683

Netherlands
De Stad Rajneesh
Cornelis Troostplein 23
1072 JJ Amsterdam
Tel.   020/5732 130
Fax   020/5732 132

Norway
Devananda
Rajneesh Meditation Center
P.O. Box 177 Vinderen
0319 Oslo 3
Tel.   02/491 590

Spain
Distribuciones "El Rebelde"
Estellencs
07192 Mallorca - Baleares
Tel.   71/410 470
Fax   71/719 027

Sweden
Madhur
Rajneesh Meditation Center
Nidalvsgrand 15
12161 Johanneshov /
Stockholm
Tel.   08/394 996
Fax   08/184 972

Switzerland
Mingus
Rajneesh Meditation Center
Asylstrasse 11
8032 Zurich
Tel.   01/2522 012

United Kingdom
Purnima Rajneesh Centre
for Meditation
Spring House, Spring Place
London NW5 3BH
Tel.   01/284 1415
Fax   01/267 1848

West Germany
The Rebel
Publishing House GmbH*
Venloer Strasse 5-7
5000 Cologne 1
Tel.   0221/574 0742
Fax   0221/574 0749
Telex 888 1366 rjtrd

Rajneesh Verlag GmbH
Venloer Strasse 5-7
5000 Cologne 1
Tel.   0221/574 0743
Fax   0221/574 0749

Tao Institut
Klenzestrasse 41
8000 Munich 5
Tel.   089/201 6657
Fax   089/201 3056

*All books available
  AT COST PRICE

AMERICA

United States
Chidvilas
P.O. Box 17550
Boulder, CO 80308
Tel.   303/665 6611
Fax   303/665 6612

Ansu Publishing Co., Inc.
19023 SW Eastside Rd
Lake Oswego, OR 97034
Tel.   503/638 5240
Fax   503/638 5101

Nartano
P.O. Box 51171
Levittown,
Puerto Rico 00950-1171
Tel. 809/795 8829

Also available in bookstores
nationwide at Walden Books

Canada
Publications Rajneesh
P.O. Box 331
Outremont H2V 4N1
Tel.   514/276 2680

AUSTRALIA

Rajneesh Meditation &
Healing Centre
P.O. Box 1097
160 High Street
Fremantle, WA 6160
Tel.   09/430 4047
Fax   09/384 8557

ASIA

India
Sadhana Foundation*
17 Koregaon Park
Poona 411 001, MS
Tel.   0212/660 963
Fax   0212/664 181

Japan
Eer Rajneesh
Neo-Sannyas
Commune
Mimura Building 6-21-34
Kikuna, Kohoku-ku
Yokohama, 222
Tel.   045/434 1981
Fax   045/434 5565

*All books available
 AT COST PRICE

For further information about Osho Rajneesh

Rajneeshdham Neo-Sannyas Commune
17 Koregaon Park
Poona 411 001, MS
India